Fly Fishing for Sales

33 Axioms

For Making Big Money in Sales

By Jim Ure

© 2014 by James W. (Jim) Ure

Gardner and Grace Publishing
Salt Lake City, Utah

www.jimurebooks.com

A percentage of the net profits from the sale of this book are split evenly between
The Henry's Fork Foundation and
Trout Unlimited

Praise for *Fly Fishing for Sales*

"Jim Ure's 33 axioms are entertaining, educational and eloquently written, and range from opening doors to eye-openers. The thought-provoking fly fishing analogies are great.

"There are valuable lessons for everyone in sales here."

>**Bert Vosters,** fly fisher and owner of Poseidon Fly Fishing Products Distribution Company, Netherlands.
>www.poseidonflyfishing.nl

"Seldom does a sales strategy book come along that provides such simple and accurate clarity on an innovative approach to enterprise selling.

"In the marketplace of today customers are conditioned to the old way of doing things and Jim Ure breaks down the process of a better way of not just selling, but of communicating with a prospect, on their terms, and in accordance with what they really want, and need.

"Having been at this business for over thirty years I found *Fly Fishing For Sales* innovative, and it did actually teach an old dog new tricks.

"I have used an advanced copy of Jim's book already, as a sales training exercise for my non-fly fishing sales professionals, to rave reviews."

>**Todd Floyd**
>Executive Vice President WW Sales and Operations
>Adaptiva, Inc.
>Bellevue, WA
>www.adaptiva.com

"Jim Ure has combined the arts of fly fishing and sales in a very interesting way. In fly fishing and sales it is necessary to know one's target and how to get them to bite. Well done!"

Maryann Townsend Ed.D.
Lindenwood University
Associate Professor of Management and MIS
Owner of MT Custom Outfitters LLC
FFF Certified Casting Instructor
CRBG Certified Custom Rod Builder

"Selling selling is not an easy task. If you have been in the sales profession forever like we have, it becomes difficult to put a new twist on the message.

"Ure has accomplished this by relating fly fishing to sales which helps the reader remember and related the lesson."

Ed Sauriol
Loan Officer
Movement Mortgage
edward.sauriol@movementmortgage.com

Cover Design by M. Sherwood Design Inc., 3310 S 2700 East #100, Salt Lake City, UT 84109. Phone (801) 484-8266

Cover photo courtesy of Steve Schmidt, Western Rivers Fly Fishers, 1071 E. 900 South, Salt Lake City, Utah, 84105. Phone 801-521-6424. http://www.wrflyfisher.com/.

Other Books by Jim Ure (James W. Ure)

Bait for Trout: Being the Confessions of an Unorthodox Angler

Hawks and Roses

Leaving the Fold: Candid Conversations with Inactive Mormons

The Laughing Trout: a Novel of Fly Fishing in a Mad, Mad World of Love and Pandemonium

In Memory of Jim Seare

Acknowledgements

Thanks especially to Jamie and Marci Omer of M. Sherwood Design whose patience and creative skills have helped make this a better book.

Many thanks to Raymond Linder, Maryann Townsend, Todd Floyd, Aaron Carpenter, Christian Dives, Bill Donovan and, Dries de Bruyn, Bert Vosters and Ed Sauriol. They read and provided critiques which also made this a better book.

Appreciation also to Alan Burrows, Steve Schmidt, Alastair Gowans and to the many other fly fishermen and women who contributed to this project, especially my Fly Fishing groups on Linkedin.

My thanks to my son Cory Ure for all the patience and intelligence he has given this project. He is a super salesman in his own right.

And to my fishing partner and brother, Joseph McCune Ure, who provides philosophical guidance and practical information. Proud to be your brother, Joe.

Some names in the case narratives of this book have been changed.

Catch and Release Means
High-Ticket Sales—Again and Again.

If You Learn the Axioms of Selling Sharp Steel Hooks to Fish, You Can Sell Anything.

All is fish that cometh to the net.
-John Heywood, *Proverbs,* written in 1546

Trout laugh. I hear them laugh every time I make a mistake when casting a fly. I imagine them deep in their runs chuckling to themselves and daring me to come and get them. On the days when I am wise, they teach me how to become a better fisher. And when I make note of what happened and apply it to my business, I become a better salesman.

Laughing trout have taught me well over 40 years of fishing and sales experience. I now share with you the lessons I have learned and the mistakes I have made. Apply these lessons and you will become a Sales Superstar. If you can sell sharp steel hooks to fish, you can sell anything.

Selling requires alertness, an agile and curious mind, exceptional knowledge of your product or service, and an awareness of the subtleties of change.** Over the years I sold large and costly concepts to the shrewdest businesses in the United States, from Procter and Gamble to wily Hollywood film producers.

The toughest initial sale I ever made was to a group of skeptical bankers, who, like wary old trout, waited patiently, reticently. Once hooked, the bankers gave me their business for the next 20 years.

Another customer, a tough, bottom-line lawyer and owner of a bottled water business, patiently resisted my lovely casts for his business. I kept returning, stalking him with new concepts until I watched his face brighten at an idea I had selected. It was exactly like presenting the right fly at the right moment. I had matched the proposal to his needs. I have been selling to this bottled water company for 26 years.

The Catch and Release Factor: If you want repeat sales, I say, "Never eat your customer." Like the trout I catch on dry flies, high ticket buyers of intangibles will come back to purchase from you again and again if you maintain a light but steady touch. As the great fly fisherman Lee Wulff once said, "Trout are too valuable to eat." And so are your customers. That is why we Catch and Release.

Your word and the service you provide are tantamount to your success in sales.

If you are selling high ticket intangibles—stocks, insurance, phone service, advertising, software, or if you are raising money for an art gallery or private school—you are selling thin air, blue sky, selling a chimera.

It is very much like selling a tiny bit of artificial fluff, feathers and sharp steel to a trout.

In fly fishing for trout there are 33 basic Axioms you can learn, every one of them applicable to selling—especially to selling high ticket, expensive items. Learn them well and become the Sales Superstar that I know is within you.

One of my first jobs was as a copy boy at a daily newspaper. I sold my way from that position to being the paper's campus correspondent at the university I was attending; then I sold the editor on my ability to move to a staff writing job.

Newspaper reporting is exciting, but publishers realize that for most news writers the rewards are psychic, not financial. I grew frustrated working for peanuts.

The following spring, immediately after graduation from college, I moved into the business world and quickly learned that sales are the heartbeat of every business, the engine that drives all enterprise.

From the junior account assistant to the president of the company, everybody is in sales.

Certain principles apply to every kind of selling, be it selling a refrigerator, selling a private jet or a selling $50 million dollar advertising campaign. A sales representative learns that the techniques for selling one product are much like selling another product.

Investment banker? Stock broker? Non-profit institution manager? You think you're not in sales? Wrong. If you are in any kind of business, account management or fund raising position today, you are in sales. And your high-ticket sales prospect offers special challenges:

1. In high ticket sales the prospects are fewer and hard to reach.
2. The sales prospect is targeted by many salesmen and women and there may be a parity between the products or services that he or she is offered.
3. The sales prospect is jaded and hardened by sales representatives who have flailed the waters time and again, often with noisy inefficiency, perhaps even repelling the prospect and leaving the waters muddied.

Your window of opportunity is tight and narrow in high ticket sales, and you must approach it with all the stealth and strategy of a stalking dry fly fisherman.

It was one of those long waits between casts. I watched the morning breeze spangle the green water with dancing sunlight. I held my rod under my arm, enjoying the moment.

Fly fishing is a meditative art. The rhythm of casting serves as a pump to clear my mind of everything but the moment I'm in. Now I was still, and watching. I was waiting for a large trout to rise. Then I would stalk him to make my presentation.

As I waited, an awareness came over me. I knew instinctively that it was time to begin this book. Forty years was long enough to wait to create the allegories linking fly fishing with business success.

When you get to Axiom 15 you will read how I made a sales presentation to the wrong guy. The weekend following this debacle I went fishing. While on the river I thought about my mistake and later I wrote it in a note to myself and slipped it into a file marked "Fishing for Business."

Most of these Axioms found their way to that file over all these years. They are all based on real situations. Some of the names and situations have been changed, for obvious reasons.

Share your sales rep and fishing stories with me? I want to hear them because I love being a salesman. Both of my grandfathers were salesmen and I wish they were here today so I could compare notes. Selling is a skill you can take anywhere. Even in the toughest of times there is a job for you somewhere. Salesmen and saleswomen are practical, tough and yet always dreaming of a better future. They are the ultimate in optimism about the human condition. And salesmen and women are the most fun people I know. Send your feedback to www.jimurebooks.com.

Axiom One: Embrace Your Business.

Surrender to the invigorating pull of the river. Be dazzled by the spangles of sunlight as the water dances on its surface. See how it parts around rocks and branches, subtly muscling from bank-to-bank. Touch your fingers to the water and taste them. Marvel at the dimpled stillness where your trout rise to feed, wary, lovely and worthy. This river of business is ever-changing, constantly renewing, forever exciting. And so is your business. Fall in love with it.

To business that we love we rise betime
And go to't with delight.
--William Shakespeare, *Antony and Cleopatra*

A Forty Year Fascination with His Business

If you are like me you have doubtless fallen in love with a certain stretch of trout water. I love the Henry's Fork of the Snake River, for instance. It contains big fish. The landscape through which it flows is absolutely beautiful. It feels *right*. I go there again and again. A business should have that same hold on you.

    Dr. Louis R. Curtis was retiring as president and CEO of a large and successful dairy products processing and packaging company with distribution throughout Western America. I invited him to lunch.

    Why have you been successful, I asked the gray haired senior? (You should ask this question to every company executive you admire).

    "It's all about falling in love with your business," he said.

    I knew that in the 1940s this company had been a small group of dairy farmers battling for their economic survival. Dr. Curtis had graduated from

Cornell and had brought his passion for dairy science to this group during the Great Depression.

"These dairymen were about to go under when I arrived," he said to me as he sipped his soup. "They were providing home milk delivery in glass bottles, using antiquated processing equipment. Worse, they didn't have a clue about modern dairy processing.

"The board of directors asked me if I would take a look at their business. The financial statements told me they were broke. Some of the farms were already in foreclosure. I wanted more than anything in the world to take this job, but I could not jeopardize my young family.

"Before making a decision I visited with their customers. The customers made one thing very clear: Milk was just milk. Price was everything. I went into the markets and looked at the coolers with row-after-row of glass bottles of milk.

"Then it came to me. While at Cornell I had seen a company demonstrate a new way to package milk--some genius had invented a paper carton that would hold the stuff.

"I called the packaging company. I told them that if they would put their equipment in our plant at no cost to my farmers, we would put all our milk production in paper cartons.

"Then I went to the farmers and told them what I had done. If they wanted me, they would have to do as I told them, and that included converting to paper cartons. There always is resistance in any company to innovation, and someone asked what good would it do?

"It will enable our customer to buy his quart of milk for a penny less than they pay for it now," I told them. Finally, they agreed to go ahead with the paper carton idea.

"Three years later we had an astounding 50 per cent of the market. My farmers were making money. The competition tried to stop us by pricking pin holes in our cartons to turn them into leakers, but within another five years most dairies had converted to paper cartons. Then we had to deal with a new kind of competition.

"For the next 40 years it was like this. One moment success, another moment a challenge. Every moment was exciting for me. No two days were the same."

In today's market, some dairies are going back to glass bottles. Recycling now gives a dairy a point of superior exclusivity in a "green-minded" culture.

If you love your business, you tend it carefully and grow it like a garden.

Axiom Two: Observe With Detachment.

Balance your excitement with the clarity that comes with perspective and detachment. Walk in the river in high water and in low water. Lift its gravels. Sift it to know what grows in it. Mark its fluctuations. Find the places where the fish hold.

The most sensitive people... are men of business and of the world, who argue from what they see and know, instead of spinning cobweb distinctions of what things ought to be.
—William Hazlitt *(1778-1830), "On the Ignorance of the Learned"*

Mark the Fluctuations

Fishing may be good, but keep an eye out for thunderstorms. A graphite rod attracts lightning.

You may become emotionally involved in your sales work yet you must maintain the detachment in order to provide yourself with the perspective to make good sales decisions.

You need to always be alert to the realities of the market, as was illustrated to me when I worked at Procter and Gamble in the Foods Division.

Our P&G cake mix group wanted to know the future of our business. At the time P&G's Duncan Hines Cake mixes had become the market leader. They had developed a formula that made the finished product moister than those of the competition.

The Food Products Division at P&G was supposedly the light of the future for the marketing giant.

What would the future for cake mixes be?

"You need to keep tabs on the fluctuations in the market, not just in your product," said Robert Kingsmith, a P&G exec as we entered the board room one morning to receive a presentation of the results of an extensive study by a well-known and highly regarded research group, Simmons.

Out came the charts as our presenter cleared his throat.

"There is good news and bad news," said the presenter. "We found that while Procter and Gamble's market share of cake mixes has grown, we also found that the overall market for cake mixes is shrinking. There is a trend toward lighter desserts." He walked us through pages of charts. They clearly demonstrated a declining market.

It was on that day that P&G got the word that it might not want to stay in the cake mix business forever, and it might want to focus on other products with a greater promise of expanding markets. Eventually P&G divested itself of the Duncan Hines label, partly to allow its sales reps to focus on brands with growth potential.

Todd Floyd, Executive Vice President WW Sales and Operations in Bellevue, Washington says it so succinctly: "Become too attached to a deal and you lose sight of the fact that it may not be profitable at all. Sometimes the risk of breaking off all of your bugs shooting for that little spot under the logjam is not worth it. Walk away."

Axiom Three: Risk It

Wade. Fall in. Be swept away. Learn from your mistakes. Surrender to win.

A company must be flexible enough to attack itself with a new idea.
—Al Ries and Jack Trout, *The 22 Immutable Laws of Marketing*

Surrender to Win

After a month as a sales representative and with some sales success, Mark thought he knew it all and now was trying to sell the lady of the house on his company's bottled water service.

He had told her about the product's superiority over that of the competition—it was pure spring water with fewer dissolved solids when compared to the competition's filtered tap water.

He had a demonstration that showed the health benefits of spring water—free of sodium, pure without chlorine. He argued that its cost was comparable to a filtration system and how water from a bottle provided a better product.

He showed her the bottled water dispenser, a model that would complement her modern kitchen, providing cold water for punch for the kids and hot water for things like tea and instant ramen noodles.

The prospect, a woman home owner, parried every thrust of the conversation with short ripostes of rejection, a simple "No."

In despair he finally said, "You aren't buying, are you."

"No, I am not."

At this moment he surrendered. "What's wrong with my spring water?"

"It's not the water. It's the dispenser. I have small children and I worry about them playing with it and burning themselves with hot water from the hot tap.

Mark had finally surrendered his ego and listened to his prospect. He left the lady and returned to the plant later in the day, telling Dave, his sales manager, of his rejection by the young mother.

"Oh," said the sales manager, brightening. "We have a dispenser model that is childproof. You have to move the taps backward and depress them before they will let the water flow. Little kids can play with them all day and nothing comes out of them."

Mark returned to the lady the next day and showed her the dispenser and its child-proof taps.

"Sign me up," said the lady.

Axiom Four: Expect To Win

You will bring a trout to the net. Hold that knowledge confidently.

When I feel like I will catch fish, I catch fish. When I feel doubtful, I never catch fish. Figure that out.
—John Young, violin maker and fisherman, personal commentary

Generating Confidence

The best salesman I ever met came into my office with his product, a financial service.

"You're a great salesman," I said, thinking of offering him a job at my own firm. "What's your secret?"

"I try to have confidence," he said modestly. "I spend 30 minutes every morning centering myself. I pray and meditate, asking for the will of a higher power to guide me.

"I ask that same higher power to provide me with confidence by keeping my expectations to a minimum. Projecting the outcome of a situation absolutely destroys my confidence because outcomes are always different than my expectations. Sometimes the real outcomes are even better than I could have imagined.

"So on my bathroom mirror I have a small sign that says:
'It ain't going to happen that way.'
"On my computer I have another small sign that says,
It ain't going to happen that way, either.'"

"I am confident I will sell you something, but I don't know what it will be. Really, it's a numbers game. You cast to enough fish, you catch one. So as long as I'm casting I am confident I will sell. In fishing, I never know if I'll hook a brown trout, a rainbow, a brook trout or even a grayling or a small-mouth."

He added, "Confidence comes to me with spiritual preparation and thorough product knowledge. I know that I am prepared to answer questions about my product because I have immersed myself in it. The sale comes, but never as I expected it to.

I made a note of his fishing metaphor. I also signed a contract with him. Couldn't touch him as an employee, however. He was making too much money where he was.

Axiom Five: Set No Time

There is no season on your trout. If he resists in summer when the hatch is strong, return in winter and drift a nymph. Patience is the mark of wisdom.

Back in the fifties the Nash Rambler was America's first small car. But American Motors didn't have the money or the courage to hang in there long enough for the category to develop.
—Al Ries and Jack Trout, *The 22 Immutable Laws of Marketing*

Coyote Beer

A guy I knew loved making beer. He carefully brewed small batches of artisan beer that he would give to friends and serve at parties. He called it Coyote Beer. It was righteous beer, as all agreed, and he was often solicited to sell the stuff.

"If I could make a living at it, I would. It was the early 1970s and the big brewers would never let me in the market," he sighed. He watched and waited.

In the 1980s, the big brewers continued consolidating, buying out small brewers until there were essentially just three giants: Anheuser Busch, Miller and Coors.

Slowly things had changed. My guy's patience had seen a consolidation that resulted in the disregard of the palates of many beer drinkers.

The big guys had become so big that little brewers creating small batches of artisan beer could develop niche markets. My guy thought maybe he could sneak in under the radar.

My guy put on his salesman's cap and visited his local supermarket. Sure, they would sell his beer. He went to other markets. He became involved in the local food movement. He created a pub where he could showcase his beer. He created off-beat beer types beside Coyote Beer.

Today Coyote Beer is one of hundreds of small, profitable and proliferating brewers who waited until the time was right. Coyote may get very big, and in time, another salesman with another idea for a beer, may come in under the radar to compete with that giant, Coyote Beer.

As craft brews gain intense followings, the demand—and even a black market—have made some brands very desirable. Five cases of Heady Topper Beer recently sold for $825 on Craigslist.

Axiom Six: Persevere

Be prepared to cast again and again.

*Many things which cannot be overcome when they are together,
yield themselves up when taken little by little.*
--Plutarch, (AD 46-120), from *Sertorius*

Sinatra's Story

In 1952 Frank Sinatra was washed up, a has-been. He'd fallen out with his agent, he lost his contract with Columbia Records where the musical director said he "couldn't give away" Sinatra's records. His fan clubs were disbanding and were even calling him "Frankie-Not-So-Hotra."

From his glorious Paramount Theater debut in 1942 with screaming bobby soxers and his top-hit popularity all through the 1940s, Sinatra had suddenly tumbled into near-oblivion.

Now he was reduced to singing in basement clubs in Philadelphia.

The public was critical of his lifestyle after he divorced his first wife, Nancy, and his new wife, the film star Ava Gardner, was all he had left. Even Ava was wavering in her support, especially since she was paying all his bills. He was broke.

Sinatra had heard that Columbia Pictures was going to make a film of James Jones's novel, *From Here to Eternity*. Sinatra thought he would be perfect for the part of Maggio and thought the part might be the ticket to his comeback. He wanted the part so ferociously that he began a sales campaign for it.

He lobbied hard for the role. He made phone calls to everyone he knew in Hollywood. He called them again and again. He went to see the fabled Harry Cohn, king of Columbia, begging for the role. Cohn thought of him as a singer, not an actor, and rejected him.

Sinatra continued to bombard Columbia executives with cables signed "Maggio." He coaxed Ava Gardner to make a call to Cohn, asking that he be screen-tested for the part.

Bombarded by calls and cables, Cohn reluctantly agreed. Sinatra was summoned for a screen test. He was in competition with at least eight other actors. He proved himself perfect for the skinny, mouthy Maggio, and Columbia cast him in the role.

From Here to Eternity premiered in August, 1953. Newsweek declared, "When the mood is on him, Sinatra can act." New Yorker magazine said he was "a first rate actor." In March, 1954, he was awarded an Oscar for Best Supporting Actor. He never looked back, achieving stratospheric success.

Sinatra's career was re-launched because of his perseverance. He became the Chairman of the Board.

Axiom Seven: Let the River Talk to You

When does your river awaken? When do your fish feed recklessly with little regard for the cost to themselves? When do your fish feed warily, exhibiting the miserly habits of a skeptic?

Observe due measure, for right timing is in all things the most important factor.
—Hesiod, (700 BC), *Works and Days*

For Everything There Is a Season

     A sales representative can learn a lot from retailers. They are attuned to the subtle nuances of the consumer psyche.
     Susan Luxton owned a boutique gift and card shop called Floribunda Bella. Her excellent taste in fabrics, design, gifts and accessories were not enough to make her store a hit. At first the little shop languished.
     A skilled reader of people and an excellent communicator, Susan established relationships with many of the women who came into her shop. This became a kind of subtle research program. She changed displays, ordered new categories of gifts, candles and stationery.
     Still, it wasn't enough.
     Her breakthrough came when she turned to her vendors for help and began attending the big gift and stationery merchandising markets in San Francisco and New York. It was her vendors who made her aware of the acute seasonality of the gift business.
     Christmas buying for retailers takes place as early as May or June, with delivery of goods coming in September or October. Spring gift orders are made in January.

Now Susan could combine her own excellent taste with suggestions made by vendors and based on orders from the year before, and on sales trends they were observing. She built a significant business and eventually sold the little shop for a surprisingly large sum.

Her vendors were keys to her success. The right product, the right place, the right price, the right questions at the right time. It will work for you, too.

As Bill Donovan tells me, this story is about listening for the cycle and then taking them steps we must take to align our perfectly-drifted blue-winged olive.

Axiom Eight: Select Your Trout

Which species will you choose?

The brown trout, crepuscular, living in deep runs as it consumes its own young, big and wary from two thousand years of international fishermen?

The rainbow, the flashy all-American acrobat, a trout of modesty that likes fast white water in a riffle or below a fall.

The brook trout, small (usually), eager, demanding, everywhere.

The cutthroat, guileless and declining, a trout with perhaps a diminishing future as he feeds at river's edge in the pocket water or dimples the surface of isolated lakes.

Each species is different; each individual within a species is different.

One size does not fit all. If you think all bottled waters are alike, you are dead wrong. Read the labels. You have your natural spring water, then comes artesian water, then you have your processed tap water, sometimes called purified water; then you have distilled water. After that there's what we see labeled as "drinking water." Next we go to the mineral water category...

—Keynote speaker, *Annual Conference*
International Bottled Water Association
Washington, D.C.,

Who Are You Selling To?

Imagine that you are the L. L. Bean Catalogue. Examine who you appeal to on each of your pages. This is a great exercise in determining which consumer to sell to.

L. L. Bean is superior at knowing who its customers are and how to sell to them.

First they deliver a general L. L. Bean catalogue. This one fishes for your interest. You'll find outdoor equipment, packs, tents, totes and organizers. Then there is footwear, from kids hiking shoes to Mom's gardening Wellingtons. And it offers clothing, from soft flannel shirts to khaki trousers and swimsuits.

The young mother reads this catalogue. Then dad picks it up. Going through this book of dreams becomes a family affair. Orders are placed.

Back at L. L. Bean in Freeport, Maine, sales managers are sifting the computerized purchase records from these catalogues, determining who is buying what, matching lifestyle, sex, age and location to products. Now they can target the family more specifically. If you order a tent, you'll get their Outdoor Gear catalogue. If you order clothing, you'll get a special catalogue of wearables. Order sheets or a comforter and you will receive the home furnishings book.

Their frequent e-mails will provide you with special offers in the categories of your interest so you can buy on-line.

Personally, I look forward to the L. L. Bean Fishing Catalogue that comes each winter, well in advance of the fishing season. This is the time that we fishers are snow-locked and thinking of the warm summer days and willow-lined brooks. It is a catalogue that sells dreams. I have noticed that I tend to buy more gear in winter, in anticipation of the season ahead. Someone at L. L. Bean knows this. That's why it arrives when it does.

Come mid-summer, we get the Home/Casual Furnishings catalogue with its promise to women of "over 150 fall favorites to warm any room." This one is for young women who want country style and good value.

L. L. Bean targets season, sex, and lifestyle activity. Because of excellent focus they can send emails and catalogues of special interest to different segments of their customer market. They have learned that if a woman buys a certain type of flannel shirt, they can almost count on her to purchase a certain corduroy trouser.

Today's marketing gorilla is Amazon. Amazon has created a state-of-the-art algorithm for knowing and showing what its customers' tastes are. Type in the name of any book, CD, DVD, or household item in which you have an interest. Up pops not only that item but several like them. They target you for cross-selling.

They know who they are fishing for and how to catch you.

Axiom Nine: Find Your Match

What is the trout's job? What is your job? Which trout fits your desires? Limit your choice and focus.

Life does not give itself to one who tries to keep all its advantages at once. I have often thought morality may perhaps consist solely in the courage of making a choice.
—Leon Blum, 1872-1950

Be Specific.

Where is the fit in fishing?

For many years my bottled water company client did very well merely by having a single good product and a horizontal market of consumers who ranged from youngsters to retirees.

Then came Coke and Pepsi. Seeing their market in soft drinks declining, Coke and Pepsi created Dasani and Aquafina bottled waters.

The soft drink giants were well aware of the subtleties of the so-called vertical markets, those consumer group niches that have distinct preferences in terms of beverages.

With their deep pockets, Coke and Pepsi expended a lot on research to determine who the heavy users of bottled water were. They isolated heavy users of bottled water and made their sales pitch to them via store shelves and advertising. The salesmen for Coke and Pepsi were selling lifestyle geared to primary users of the product. Suddenly, the bottled water market had been fractured and changed for ever.

Faced with the challenge of these two giants, the local bottled water companies either sold out as the industry consolidated, or it redoubled efforts, as my client did.

My client learned to identify specific users and to develop line extensions of our products to appeal to them.

Little kids like spring water with sweetening. We created a drink called Kwencher, which enjoyed success as a low calorie, high flavor spring water product. Mothers liked it because it was sugar-free, and because the young family market had become extremely health-conscious.

Career women are going for electrolyte-added waters that contribute to a healthy lifestyle. We created a new "health water" called Ascent for them.

In our market, research shows that younger women like plain spring water. We pitch our sales efforts to offer our classic product to them.

You can't have it all, although some companies try to be everything to everyone and frequently fail to do a good job at anything. I ask my clients to focus their sales efforts where they know they can produce results. I ask them to know what they are fishing for.

Axiom Ten: Competition Muddies the Water

Who wants your trout? Your fellow fishermen are the greatest threat to your success, for they will muddy the water. Watch them carefully. Make note of their behavior. List their character assets. Observe their techniques. Discard their poor habits. Look at their equipment. Watch where they go. Go where they do not go. Be there first.

I don't mind sharing trout with the bears and pelicans but if Redford's movie crew shows up I'm out of here.
--Zeke McCabe, photographer, *personal commentary upon reaching a certain Western trout stream.*

You can still find fish in troubled waters
—Proverb.

Go Where They Do Not Go.

Your competition is never going away. You can get to the river earlier than they do, or you can fish different waters.

I believe in getting there early. By that, I mean getting to my prospect with information more quickly than my competitors.

For instance, a group of beef ranchers in the West were considering producing a branded beef, going direct to the consumer rather than selling their cattle through the industrial beef production system.

I realized that I was able to share some market information as a result of some prior research. I called them the morning I heard they were considering this move.

They put me in touch Dee Von Bailey, a professor of economics at a highly-regarded Western university with emphasis in agriculture. Dr. Bailey wrote my firm into a grant solicitation, and the university was awarded a few months later. We got a nice piece of business out of it and generated some excellent relationships. These will eventually result in more business, I'm sure of it.

Provide solid, double-checked information the prospect can use to ensure success. This means staying informed and sharing your information.

Never call a prospect with nothing to say. Let me say this again: Never call a prospect with nothing to say or offer. That is NOT building a relationship. They are tired of hearing vendors tell them they just wanted to "check in." You are wasting their time. Always have something to give them. Add value to your conversation.

Axiom Eleven: Package Your Ideas

What does the trout *need*? Protein. What does he *want*? Protein in a delicious package. Packaging is everything.

They say the egg is nature's ultimate package—sturdy, beautifully shaped, elegantly tinted. By those standards I'd vote for Ava Gardner.
—Sheridan Andreas Mulholland Anderson, *personal commentary while fishing Curtis Creek, another isolated Western trout stream.*

The Presentation

The Ski Utah account was up for grabs. For our young and largely untested advertising and marketing agency, the account could provide the high profile our business needed in order to expand.

We officed in a building with another advertising agency. It was much older agency, considerably bigger, with prestigious clients. They wanted that account and were willing to go to any lengths to get it.

On the day we were to make our proposals to the ski organization's board of directors, we watched our big competitor's executives leave the building to make their presentation before we did. We gulped. They were wearing ski outfits! Why hadn't we thought of that?

No use worrying about it now. We were due to make our presentation in another hour. Our small crew was tense and excited and we rehearsed our roles and lines once again.

We had always been told by the big guys that we should never speculate in making presentations. Being young and without much of a track record, we had decided we had to take the risk of speculating. While I tried to display the confidence of a leader, I was by no means certain. Our proposal would either make us or break us.

We arrived at the appointed hour in our suits and ties. A dozen men and women stared at us expectantly.

We laid out our strategies. We charted our media buys, mostly in vertical market magazines where we could be certain of reaching skiers efficiently.

And then we unveiled our make-or-break package: We had written and produced three speculative advertisements that included the client's logo and slogan, The Greatest Snow on Earth. Then we had them bound into copies of Ski and Skiing magazines exactly as they would appear in a press run—exactly as a reader would see them.

The board held the magazines and looked at our ads. They murmured, glancing at one another. Was it a hit or a miss? We retired and nervously waited as the other six ad agencies made their proposals.

It was early evening when a phone call informed us we had won the account. The champagne corks popped. It was a good feeling to gamble and win, and more important, it put our little firm on the map. It would grow and prosper for many years.

Packaging was the key. Our competition packaged its people. We packaged our ideas. We packaged our presentation in a way that hooked them.

Axiom Twelve: Always Ask

Ask others the lessons they have learned from the trout and the river. Questions are not an admission of inadequacy; they are the way of enlightenment. Humans become bigger when asking questions. You could learn that in Italy they fish for trout with strawberries.

Education…is hanging around until you've caught on.
—Robert Frost

What Are You Using?

This is my most frequently asked question on any river I fish, especially when someone is consistently getting strikes while I am not!

Our egos sometimes demand that we figure it out ourselves, although the simpler, more direct way is to ask (an amazing concept).

Mel Jensen, a real estate developer with whom I had worked numerous times in the past, asked me to bid on a new project. An old acquaintance, I thought I knew his business quite well. I'd watched him build a significant niche in the townhouse market.

I made my pitch to him, a written proposal complete with a draft of a budget and strategies for reaching his market of Baby Boomers.

A week later I called him and asked if he'd made a decision.

"Yes. I'm going with your competitor."

"Why?" I know I sounded surprised, if not shocked. I thought it was a lock.

"They did more homework, Jim."

I took Mel to lunch and pumped him for more information.

"You took me for granted. I expected that you would come to me and ask more questions about this new project. If so, you'd have learned that it was targeted to a downscale, younger market, and that we needed a different selling proposition. Your pitch, frankly, was tired and not very thoughtful."

Now I try to spend exploratory time with my sales prospect prior to making the actual pitch. I ask them what they are trying to solve. There is value in creating a relationship, and there is also great value in asking just the right question, the question that can make or break the bite.

Axiom Thirteen: Calmness Endures

If you are defeated this day, move on with grace and good will.

*I said I was going to do business with the competition.
He (The losing salesman) put up a disgusting fuss.*
—John Klas, *a banker*

Memory Lingers On.

His name was Don Gray and he was a sales manager for KMOR radio, which had recently switched to a country and western format.

As far as I was concerned KMOR was a new and untried entity. Radio stations must build audience over time. I was not prepared to invest any of my banker client's money in his station for our Visa campaign.

Don Gray called the client directly, whining, putting up a fuss and trying to make points against the competition and impugning the decision of my agency. My banker client said, "We're going with our agency's decision."

That night Don called me. First, I was miffed that he called me at home. Second, he was drunk. Third, he told me I *had* to buy a flight on his station. Fourth, he told me I was stupid if I did not buy air time from KMOR.

He didn't last long at KMOR.

However, I never forgot this. I admit to the character defect of not being more charitable to the man, but the memory of this intrusion had seared itself into my brain. It colored my view of this man and his sales technique to such a degree that I could never get past his personality.

It is a living reminder that I will not always win a sale (or catch a trout), and that in loss I must ask myself what I learned and what I enjoyed about the experience.

As Todd Floyd reminded me: "More times than I can count I have gone back to a client after a loss to ask them how they are doing with the chosen solution, only to hear that 'it is not going so well'. And I get to cast again as I did not stir up the water."

Axiom Fourteen: Share What You Know—Up To a Point

Always share tactics, for they are apparent to anyone who takes the time to observe.

> *El pez muere por la boca*
> (The fish dies because he opens his mouth).
> —Spanish proverb.

Strategy is another matter.

Fishermen and fisherwomen tend to share everything they know about the fish, the river, and the patterns. This is not always a good habit to carry into your professional life in sales.

Susan Marie Solomon is a sales representative for a communications company. She told me this story.

After a presentation to a major U.S. corporation based in Los Angeles, the sales reps from the various competitive companies had gathered around a table in the hotel bar for shop talk.

Sales reps, our brothers and sisters in arms, have the odd ability to put down their natural competitiveness and willingly share tips and war stories. This night was no exception. The talk was friendly and warm, full of conversation, experiences and suggestions, punctuated by lots of laughter.

"The biggest help to me that night was in comparing sales techniques with some of the others," said Susie. "I learned a lot from Jeff, who is the rep for my biggest competitor. For instance, he told me how he planned his work day, doing triage by accepting his most important calls as they came in, and by waiting to return his other calls twice a day, just before noon and again at 4 p.m.

"Jeff also told me about his techniques for opening a conversation while making a cold call. He told me to always introduce myself and without pausing, ask the recipient of the call if they are having a good day (not, "is this a good time to talk?"). That was a good suggestion. I use it all the time.

"Meanwhile, one of the other reps, Karen, was talking openly about a new calling plan her company was going to introduce. She took a kind of pride of authorship in helping develop the plan and I guess she needed to brag a little.

"I glanced at Jeff as Karen told about the plan. It was as if he was writing down her comments. I could see him absorbing what she said.

"The upshot was that within a few days, Jeff's company had created a new calling plan that essentially spiked Karen's company's plan. Boy, did I get a lesson out of that cocktail hour."

When Susie and Jeff had talked about how to plan your business day or cold call, they were talking tactics that were useful to the daily tasks of a sales representative. When Karen divulged a corporate program, she was revealing a strategy that should have remained within the walls of her corporation.

The moral of this story is that you don't have to tell anyone about your favorite fishing place.

Axiom Fifteen: Always Cast to the Biggest Trout

Choose the biggest fish in the pod. Observe him vigilantly. Make sure he is the right choice.

See the right man at the right time.
—Italian proverb.

Decision makers don't need to talk it over with anyone.
—Jeffrey Gitomer, *Little Red Book of Selling*

Eat This Coupon

I was fishing to forget. Just a day earlier I had made a sales presentation to a prospective client, a dairy cooperative we'll call Mountain High Dairy. Working with Don, the dairy's vice president of marketing, I had spent two months researching, refining and creating a strategy.

My assignment had been twofold: create a New Year kickoff for fluid milk and cultured products and second, an ice cream campaign. The fluid milk and cultured product campaign was by far the biggest part of the budget, so I worked hard to develop the headline: *The Thing You Got for Xmas You Can't Return Is Those Extra Pounds.*

The ice cream campaign, to be kicked off later, was based on *Eat this Coupon*, an offbeat approach to a product discount.

The result? I won the little ice cream account and lost the big fluid milk account. The reason? The president of the company, devoutly religious, considered the use of the word "Xmas" to be a sacrilege. When I finally got to meet the president to explain that Xmas could easily be replaced with the word Christmas, he had already given the work to another firm.

Ironic, I thought as I watched the river boiling with small fish. My business presentation was like my fishing on that day: I went for the big one and instead caught the little one. So I made a rule:

Always cast to the biggest fish.

I had dealt with the vice president when I should have been dealing with the president of the dairy. It was a lesson I never forgot. Go for the biggest fish. I will not take shortcuts.

Axiom Sixteen: Get Close

Go to your fish whenever possible. Consume the river with him. Let him become accustomed to your body in the water. Allow him to know you.

*I didn't join the Country Club for the food or golf.
I joined to make connections.*
--Anon

Creating Relationships

I had become acquainted with Al Russo when we were members of the same duck club on the marshes of Great Salt Lake.

Al's hobby was training Labrador retrievers for field trials. There was no one who had more knowledge of these happy, loveable gun dogs. Al became well-known when one of his dogs became a grand champion at the national field trial.

In his professional life, Al Russo was very successful pharmaceutical salesman. When Al called on doctors they knew that not only was Al a good sales rep, but they also remembered him because of his high profile in the field trialing of Labrador retrievers.

Almost every time he came to the duck club he brought with him guests who were doctors, purchasing agents or hospital administrators, people with whom he did business.

He cemented his relationships with his customers during the day's hunting in a duck blind. In the evening, sitting around the fireplace, they talked business over drinks. It was a pleasant ambiance for in which to build relationships.

Over cocktails one evening he told me, "Become known for something. I don't care if it's in bowling or softball or curling. Become a club golfer. Become the president of the United Way. Pick something you like, something you feel strongly about. When someone thinks that they need a new truck or insurance or pharmaceuticals, your name pops into the front of their mind. They call you first."

Al died a few years ago, retired and wealthy and with a Labrador retriever at his bedside.

Love what you do, do what you love. And if it's fly fishing, be known for it.

Axiom Seventeen: Use the Right Rod

Are you using just enough rod? Too much and your cast will be sloppy. Too little and you will never reach your trout in a heavy wind. Take two rods. Maybe three, because rods can break. Be ready to change, depending on conditions.

You never know when the computer will go down again.
—A Qwest operator, commentary while trying to connect a conference call.

You brought duct tape?
—The Author, *to an assistant who was able to quickly and seamlessly repair a model's clothing during a commercial shoot.*

How Would You Like It Done?

I was preparing a sales proposal a large national non-profit organization. I had received a personal call from the CEO, a distant acquaintance that dated back to a time when we were both doing some community service. He told me he felt they needed a greater public profile in order for them to raise more funds. They were committed to the more than 4,000 communities they served.

We went to work creating a plan. My people labored long and hard to create a program which included a public service advertising campaign and an integrated publicity and public event series.

I wrote the proposal using the data we had collected. It ran nearly 35 pages, with charts and budgets. I asked my staff to prepare a Power Point presentation. Four of us arrived a few minutes before our appointed time. As we waited I asked the CEO's Administrative Assistant to ask how many people would be attending the presentation, since I wanted to provide a pass-out of the written proposal that they could follow as we did the PowerPoint. .

"DON"T do a PowerPoint and DON'T give him a lengthy written proposal," she whispered to me. "I have seen him practically throw people out of his office who came in loaded down with all that stuff.

"He wants a verbal presentation. He wants it quick and succinct, and then let him ask questions. Do not take more than 10 minute giving him the gist of your proposal. And go in alone." I told my own people to wait for me and I went into his office.

It was later pointed out to me that when you take an army, the client may think his work will require and army. An army of people automatically conveys—*expensive*.

We sat down on his office sofa. He poured me a coffee. I began my pitch and ran only slightly longer than the recommended 10 minutes.

"I like it. We are increasing our budget to do this. I want you to go meet with my V.P. of Development and provide him with the details. I think we'll do business with you."

This brief pitch became a significant piece of business worth over a million dollars a year. For me, it was a lesson in being prepared. There was another factor that played into the success required by this change: I knew the material in the presentation.

Another lesson from this experience: I try to get to know secretaries and administrative assistants before I make a pitch.

In preparing to shoot your line, pay attention to the conditions around you, including trees and brush that might snag your back-cast.

Axiom Eighteen: Keep Your Equipment Ready

Clean your line. Inspect for frayed areas and straighten leader kinks. Adjust reel tension. Are your knots tight? Are they the *right* knots?

> *Practice makes perfect.*
> —Proverb

> *The client's name was spelled wrong every single place it appeared in the proposal.*
> —Jim Seare, vice president,
> Axelsen Advertising Agency, Inc.,
> *Lamenting over drinks.*

Keep It Simple, Stupid.

He was a nice dog, an Alsatian I believe. We were creating a logotype for an insurance company that featured an ever-vigilant dog.

We had been asked to make a presentation to the sales representatives of the company, something to liven the meeting and inspire them to greater effort.

My vice president, the late Jim Seare, had suggested we bring the model dog to the sales meeting of the insurance company. It seemed like a good idea.

We had taken pictures of our model dog when we created the logo. He was an amiable beast, taken to sleeping most of the time. I never dreamed he could come alive as he did.

Jim waited outside the door as I introduced the new media program to the sales reps.

"And now, meet Buck, your new symbol of Surety National," I shouted happily.

And as the image of the new logo flooded the screen on stage, Jim opened the doors at the back of the little theater. Every head turned. Seare was tugging hard on the Alsatian, which was resolute in its determination not to enter the big, scary room with all the people in it.

It got worse. Seare's pulling on the dog's leash seemed to aggravate the pooch. He twisted and jumped like a hooked rainbow trout, yanking my small-statured partner almost off his feet. The dog pulled back on all fours and his head slipped through the collar. Finding himself free, the dog was off like a shot, racing through the insurance company building like someone had set his tail on fire.

It became apparent after a minute that Buck would not be led through the crowd of sales reps as a symbol of our company being the customer's steady friend. The tempo of my presentation was now broken and I had to listen to the snickers of the sales reps and the throat-clearings of the company president.

Outside the theater doors we could hear the banging of doors and the clatter of falling items as Jim Seare was joined by secretaries and staff in an attempt to capture the crazed animal.

The lesson: don't over-think your pitch. The other lessons I learned in sales:

- Always take your own AV equipment
- Always have back-up AV equipment
- Always take someone who knows how to operate the equipment
- Always take spare marking pens
- Always take an extra pad of paper in case all your AV stuff, including the backup, crashes. I've had power go out
- Check and check again any names you are spelling out in the proposal, and any titles
- Always take duct tape
- Never work with animals

It's a lot like your fly fishing equipment: maintain it in good condition and keep spares or duplicates. Always take an extra rod and reel. Otherwise, you can ruin your day before you ever get on the water.

Axiom Nineteen: Make Yourself Ready

Study your prospect. Ask them what they are trying to accomplish. Try to project what lies ahead.

I loved the business until I got into it.
—Anonymous Hollywood Producer

Businesses Are Made Up of Fallible People

Once there was a man I will call Bruce Donaldson. I'd known Bruce in social situations and had even enjoyed a fishing weekend with Bruce on the Henry's Fork of the Snake River, where he proved to be an amusing companion.

Bruce became executive director of a federal marketing project, I was happy for him. When this project came up for bid, I was delighted as its board of directors awarded my firm the account. I thought it would be a pleasure working with Bruce.

Wrong. Bruce turned out to be a misery to work with. He was uncommunicative. In fact, the man was downright secretive. If he was getting feedback from his board we never heard about it.

He did not understand that it takes a collaborative effort to make marketing work. He was confrontational, focused on fixing blame rather than fixing problems. He did not listen well. We had to pry answers to questions out of him. He talked out of both sides of his mouth, blaming our firm for problems that he stayed mum about when dealing with us.

Everyone in my firm hated having to deal with Bruce and his way of doing business. The day I announced we were dumping the account, cheers resonated in the halls of our office.

A competitor of mine came to me after his firm had taken over Bruce's account.

"What is wrong with this guy Bruce? I have never had such difficulty with an account, ever. The man's a Neanderthal at business, but a nice guy socially."

I told him we had the same problems with Bruce. We agreed on one thing: life was too short for any more of Bruce.

Many business personalities are difficult. We learn to deal with their styles. But some business people are impossible. I do not like fishing for trout and catching bottom feeders instead. Avoid doing business with them, or resign their business and don't look back. Money is not the sole purpose of your being in sales. Peace of mind comes with having boundaries.

Axiom Twenty: Do a Last Minute Check

Has the weather changed? Is the river up? Are my trout still in waiting?

I should have called to confirm the appointment.
—A television sales representative, upon learning his client had left for the day.

Find a Friend in the Company.

So much can happen between your information-gathering first meetings and the day you make your sales presentation.

We were once one of a dozen advertising and marketing firms asked to bid on the collateral material being prepared to pre-sell condominiums at a large ski resort in the Wasatch Mountains.

In our initial meeting the developer, Jens Allred, an athletic man with a strong personality, described the market he wanted as being upscale residents who lived in major metropolitan areas in California, areas easily accessible to the Wasatch via Salt Lake International Airport.

We went to work on creating our strategy. I wrote copy and worked with my creative director to execute the message. Our media whiz, Annie Sondrup, researched the efficient use of the budget. Los Angeles and San Francisco were our target markets, and we had found cost-effective and timely ways to reach the upscale ski traveler in both markets.

Randy Williams, a colleague and long-time ski pal, was working at the fledgling resort and was peripheral to the planned campaign. He called me.

"I called to tell you I think there are some changes afoot. We now have a single large investor interested in buying the whole condo project from Jens. This guy's swimming in Texas oil money. He will be sitting in on the presentation you make to Jens. You might want to re-think your strategy."

"How's that?" I asked.

"Think Texas. He's talking pretty loud about the Texas market."

We had just two days until the presentation. I called in my team. We reviewed the creative work. We had to tweak it to modify the travel time to Salt Lake International, but otherwise the creative message would hold up well for the Texans. And Texas looked like a pretty good market. Annie researched the Texas ski clubs and began isolating media buys.

On the day of the presentation we marched in and set up our stuff. Shamelessly I announced to Jens that we had done as he had told us regarding the California market, but that we also wanted him to look at the possibility of going into Texas markets. And just look at this, our media buyer has created an additional plan for Dallas-Ft. Worth, Austin and Houston.

We got the business. We got a bigger budget. And I learned to always try to find someone inside the company who can (1) provide you with inside information and (2) become a sounding board you can call with your ideas before you actually present them. People love to be asked for advice. Try it today. "I would like to ask your advice on…"

It's like calling the local fly shop in order to be better prepared.

Axiom Twenty One: Be Healthy and Centered As You Can Be

Make sure you are as well as you can be. Eat and drink lightly. Take deep breaths at the river. Maintain your balance. You have come a long way in order to stand at the river's edge, and good health has brought you to this moment. Let gratitude fill your mind.

> *It's a great advantage not to drink among hard-drinking people.*
> *You can hold your tongue and moreover,*
> *you can time any little irregularity of your own*
> *so that everybody else is so blind that they don't see or care.*
> —F. Scott Fitzgerald, *The Great Gatsby*.

Clarity of Mind and Soul

If you make a sales call hung-over and thick-minded, your odds drop by half. If you make a pitch while you are high, they drop by two-thirds. Please believe me.

Most successful people are moderate in their habits. Save the drinks for the after-sale party. For some of us to be successful, total abstinence may be necessary.

Looking back in my hard-partying years, cocktails at lunch inevitably drifted into cocktails before dinner, then wine with dinner, maybe a little brandy after.

Some business men and women can function like this. I could not.

More than once I made presentations after three-martini lunches. This was a common occurrence when I first started in business. I am glad to say that this is far less common today than it was then. (Cocaine, methamphetamine and other drugs are present today as anodynes for harried salesmen and women and both are just as mind-junking as booze). I know men and women who destroyed their careers with alcohol and other substances.

    I had a few clients whose common practice was to do business over drinks. Proposals I made while high were disastrous. My responses were muddled and slow.

    When I had a few beers while fishing, my casts were sloppy and my hook sets were too late. I was also prone to fall in the river and have my waders fill with water, which I once did because I didn't want to lose the beer in my hand.

Axiom Twenty Two: Step into Changing Water

No matter how well you have prepared, understand that some things will change, for change is inevitable. Stay flexible. Stay alert. Have plenty of backing on your reel.

What would you do if we told you we only had half our original budget?
What would you do if I told you we were going to double the budget?
—Marketing Director at Western ski resort advertising presentation

More Depth Than You Need.

Once in a while, making a sale will take you on the ride of your life. You better be prepared to set the hook, no matter how slow the fishing has been.

What started as a simple term life insurance sale turned into the sale of the century for J.D. Case. He had made a call on a low-profile businessman named Arleigh Anderson.

Arleigh had a shabby office in an aging downtown building with flyspecked windows. Shelves creaked under sheaves of files thick with dust. The old wooden swivel chair J.D. was invited to sit in appeared to be a relic from the 1930s.

Arleigh was flinty and cheap. He had made a fortune in mining back in the days when lead, zinc and silver produced a handsome income.

Arleigh had called J.D. because he'd seen a small advertisement J.D. ran every Sunday in the business pages of the daily newspaper.

"I want a little insurance," he had told J.D.

On this day J. D. was prepared to write the term policy he had been asked about, a modest $100,000 policy "To help buy a memorial and bury me," Arleigh said.

They worked up the details. Abruptly, Arleigh Anderson said, "What do you know about estate planning?" J.D. had recently completed a financial planning course and was conversant in estate planning. He began by asking questions, then told Arleigh he would return with answers. J.D. developed a relationship with Arleigh based on his knowledge of the products available to him. He had knowledge the man admired, and he was able to find a fit between Arleigh and the man's desires.

The rest of the story is that Arleigh turned over to J.D. all the financial planning for his $40 million dollar estate. Arleigh's estate has been the major contributor to J.D.'s own wealth, which today is not insignificant.

When J.D. called on this low profile businessman he did not expect to catch a big sale. In business and fishing, things are not always as they seem. Stay flexible. Stay alert. Have plenty of backing on your reel; you never know when you might be pleasantly surprised with a big fish.

Axiom Twenty Three: Slow Is Real

Stalk your trout slowly, a single step a minute, waiting at each movement to let him accept your vibration and to accommodate it.

All human errors are of impatience,
a premature breaking off of methodical procedure...
—Franz Kafka, *Collected Aphorisms*

Wait and See.

    Be wary of the prospect who is too eager to buy. These people may be comparable to trout with whirling disease. There is a likelihood they are not what they seem. Unscrupulous people lurk everywhere, especially in business.
    Any solid deal—especially if it is a big deal—is usually going to take time to develop and close.
    A man named Lawler called my advertising and marketing agency to a meeting at a hotel. We arrived, shook hands, and began getting acquainted with Lawler and his two partners, Stan and Ollie. It turned out that they were all local. So why were we meeting them at a hotel?
    My suspicions began to deepen. Meeting at an office was more businesslike, although I frequently have met in a client's home. I sensed they were trying to present themselves as something they really were not.
    They were going to build a high rise condominium on Majorca, in the Balearic Islands of Spain. Now that's a long way from home, but okay, what can we do for you?

They needed an elaborate website, brochure and other collateral material. In fact they had even worked up sketches of exactly how they wanted it, so we wouldn't even have to have our "drawing guy" work on it much. And of course they needed it fast, since people were clamoring to buy units in their Majorca condominiums.

Lawler literally pushed the design at me and asked how soon we could get it to the printer. Something was wrong here. I was getting a bad vibe.

I said I would have to think about it.

"What's to think about? We're giving you the business. Start now."

"Okay, I'll need an up-front payment."

"No. We'll pay you when the printing is delivered."

"Good luck on finding someone to help you," I said.

I felt like I was a trout being stalked. Some customers want to work on your money. It is better karma to walk away without the sale.

Axiom Twenty Four: Watch for Patterns

The trout rises to sip an insect, and then drops to the river bottom. Another rise, a swirl of a dorsal fin. A third time his mouth breaks the surface. He is focused and feeding and ready for your fly.

You can tell when the machine is ready to jackpot.
There's a hum in the air. It's instinctive.
—Larry Horton, a realtor visiting Las Vegas
after winning $6,000 on his third pull on a slot machine.

The Benefits of Patience and Service

I frequently get calls making inquiries about costs of our services. These are like the trout that has been bumping your fly all morning but never quite makes a strike.

Often the inquiries are from small businessmen and women who are curious. They are the "lookee-loos" that every business gets, people who are "just thinking about it." Truth is, they want to know one thing: how much will it cost?

I used to be dismissive of such calls. They took up time. You could never give them the pat answer they wanted because there are so many variables. Slowly I came to understand that while most of them would never be customers, one of them might become an account that I valued.

I adopted a philosophy: *spend whatever time a caller wants, answer any questions that I can.* Most lookee-loos choked and said "thank you" and hung up when the heard the cost of today's typical advertising and marketing campaign.

Just as important, however, was that by talking to not-so-good prospects it enabled me to hone my company message, to better understand who we were, to research questions that I might never have had answered, and to perform a service for a small business that it might never have been able to afford.

I chalk it up to giving something back. I went on about my business, seldom if ever hearing any more from them.

One man, however, kept calling over a period of a couple of years. His name was Jerry DeLuca and he had retired from the nearby Air Force base and wanted to start a small business making replacement screens for homes. I suggested he use the phone for direct calling to generate leads to start with. I also had him install new screens at my home.

A few months later Jerry called again. He was enjoying some success with his screen replacement business. How would he go about approaching bigger customers, apartment complexes, for instance?

I wrote up some text for a series of what we called mini-mailers, index card sized mailers with just enough copy to get him remembered. We mailed them and the return on investment was very good.

Jerry now had a number of major apartment complexes calling him for screens. Finally, Jerry got a very big contract to provide screens for government projects in the West. He has me handle his contractor-relations and sales programs and we also put out a newsletter for Jerry. This campaign has helped grow a multi-million dollar business. Who knew? Beside that, I really like the guy.

The point is that you never know when a customer may finally be ready to strike. How many times have I heard a sales rep say "This goofy-looking guy just kept coming back. Then he surprised me. He actually bit."

Axiom Twenty Five: Find a Unique Selling Proposition

Your fly must be perfect for this moment on this water, a fly uniquely suited to your trout. Your selection of a fly is the essence of all your skill, representing the idea that brings you to this moment.

The Unique Selling Proposition (USP...) must be one that the competition either cannot, or does not, offer.
—Rosser Reeves, *Reality in Advertising*

Nobody Else is You

A trout is selecting flies from among a huge number of insects that dance and drift on the water. Why should it take mine?
Why should you buy from me? What makes my business different and better than any other? Find what makes your product or business have <u>superior exclusivity</u>. Create it through experience, experimentation or research.

- You have a superior filter in the vacuum you sell.
- The clothes washer-dryer line you represent is guaranteed longer, with fewer breakdowns.
- You have a computerized program for predicting mutual fund cycles that has a track record of 74% accuracy.

- Your computer programs are proven to crash less frequently.
- Only your charity serves a certain population of the needy.
- You have a nicotine-free cigarette (yes, it's been tried).
- You have created a mix of insurance types that provide a coverage unique in the industry.
- Your soft drink has lots of flavor with less sugar.
- Your resort is easier to get to, so you can spend more time on vacation.
- Your cell phone plan offers more free minutes.
- Your title company offers free pickup and delivery.
- Your real estate firm provides home-owner warranties for any buyer for one year at no cost.
- Your auto brand has a sensing device to warn against backing-up collisions.
- Your mutual fund has shown double digit growth for five years in a row.

You can find something superior in whatever you sell, or you can design it into the product or service. It takes strategic thinking to do it. It's what makes your selling a sure thing. Remember, lower price is NOT superior exclusivity that lasts. Anybody can give their products away.

The bottom line: Do what they <u>do not</u> do. Your fly must be a unique fit for the fish you stalk. Start differentiating your fly fishing by studying the insect cycle on your favorite body of water.

Axiom Twenty Six: Deliver Honestly

Two false casts only (or maybe none). Shoot the line. Mend its belly expertly and quickly, taking the slack from your presentation. Your line must be an extension of your confidence.

Speech is power; speech is to persuade, to convert, to compel.
It is to bring another out of his bad sense into your good sense.
—Ralph Waldo Emerson, *Letters and Social Aims*

Make Every Cast Count

I got a call from a fellow named Robert Blakemore. He had a new publication, a magazine called BizWest, directed to business executives in a large Western U.S. market.

Robert gave me his pitch. BizWest had not printed its first copy, yet he told me how it would reach upscale managers who make decisions. He said it would be glossy and attractive. He quoted me a price for an ad.

I told him no. I said that I would keep an eye on his publication with a mind to watching how it developed. I wished him well.

Robert called me the next day. Now he had lowered the price of an ad. But wait, there's more! Buy one ad, get another insert free the following month. I told him no again. I repeated my concerns: it was a new publication. I was not committing any of our clients' budget to his book.

The third call was at 6:45 a.m. to my home phone. It was his biggest mistake. I hadn't had my first cup of coffee.

Here is what he said: "If you don't buy an ad, BizWest might fail before it even gets started." He was digging his hole deeper by his bullying and guilt-tripping. He nailed the lid on the coffin when it was apparent the publication was undercapitalized.

When making your sales calls, make each one count. Like a fine cast, your pitch should be smooth and confident, expressing certainty about the quality of your product or service.

Axiom Twenty Seven: Deliver Naturally, Execute Simply

Allow your fly to take a natural drift, without drag or interference. Trust your fly to coax desire from the waiting trout. Be still and observe.

> *Nothing astonishes men so much as common sense and plain dealing.*
> —Ralph Waldo Emerson, *The essay "Art"*

Beautiful To Watch

Your well-presented fly is analogous to a complete proposal. When is a proposal complete? When a prospect stops asking questions. Your formal presentation should be just the prelude.

A great cast puts the fly exactly where it belongs, and the perfect question invites the response that you want to answer. These answers differentiate your product in the mind of the prospect.

I accompanied a salesman named Jamie Gillmor on his calls one day. Jamie is a sheep rancher who with his wife Linda own Morgan Valley Lamb, an esteemed brand found in exclusive Western resort restaurants and upscale natural food markets.

On this day Jamie was introducing a new natural branded line of beef called Boulder Mountain Beef.

He literally sold the sizzle, not the steak.

"Here we have a prime beef, locally produced. It's the best grilling beef I've eaten in years because it has that old fashioned beef flavor that the giant cattle processing business has gotten away from."

He told them where the beef was raised, in a rural part of south-central Utah. He said the ranchers who produced it grazed their cattle in the columbines and pines on the high mountains in the summer, and then brought them down to lower elevations where they were tended in private, fenced pastures, not feedlots.

He explained to them this was beef the ranchers raised and set aside for their own families. Knowing exactly when to stop, he waited expectantly. It was their turn now. He was finished with his casting. The questions started pouring out:

Q: "Grass finished?"

A: "Pasture grass and grain finished," said Jamie.

Q: "Is it organic?"

A: "No. It qualifies as natural beef. It is raised without hormones or antibiotics."

Q: "Where are they processed?"

A: "A USDA certified plant in Castle Dale."

Q: "Can we get it fresh?"

A: "Yes. Fresh or frozen. Cryovac packaged or in primals. Your choice.

Q: "Price?"

At this point Jamie gave them the price list, which included a recapitulation of the benefits and attributes.

The beauty in watching this was Jamie's timing. He had shot his line into the place where the fish were holding. He answered every question fully and concisely. It was an exciting pleasure to watch the fish rise.

Axiom Twenty Eight: Enjoy the Take

The "take" is trout fishing's most exquisite instant. Your quarry says *yes*, the most beautiful word in any language. The fish takes the fly. Your line tightens your heart thunders.

He who kisses the Joy as it flies
Lives in Eternity's sunrise.
—William Blake

You Have A Sense.

As you watch your fly drift, there comes a moment when you know a strike is imminent. The fly dances on the surface, but a sixth sense tells you a trout is about to take it. Suddenly comes that explosion and the rings of water extend outward from your fly.

During your sales pitch, you get the exact same feeling at some point. The prospect has not said anything to you. She's still listening. It may be indicated by a nod, an intake of breath, a resettling in the chair behind the desk. Body language.

Then you hear, "Okay. I think we'll do it. Yes."

I have been known to grow faint at this moment in the pitch. I am flustered and don't quite know what to say. I've been building up to this point but now I am tongue-tied. Shall I do a touchdown dance? Or whoop loudly?

Today I respond by saying, "I'm glad. I think you are going to be very pleased." I do this because I am now entering a new phase of the process of selling to my customer. I have to keep in mind that just because I have heard the word "yes," there is still much critical work to come.

Care for your customer was you would care for a fish you have just hooked.

Axiom Twenty Nine: Never Set the Hook Too Hard

Some trout hook themselves as they turn from the surface. Insure a good set with a deft turn of the wrist. Too hard a set and you'll snap the leader and the trout will leave with your fly. Feel your trout for the right set. Let your senses tell you.

The assaying of tea is an art and not a science.
It is the man, and not his instruments, which is the most important.
There can be no substitute for my experience and intuited knowledge.
—Timothy Mo, *British novelist*

No Time to Rest Now

The period after "yes, I'll buy," is akin to setting the drag on your reel. There is still the glow of happiness between buyer and seller.

There are intermediary questions that you should be ready to ask of your customer-to-be. Try to nail everything down in order to get ready for the play ahead.

I watched a woman with the unlikely name of Ruby Custer sell $200,000 in laser surgery equipment to a group of doctors with an ophthalmic practice.

The equipment she offered would be good for their practice. During the sale Ruby had focused on showing them, via a laptop demonstration, not how the instrument worked, but how it would produce profits based on a per-patient use, how it would free up more time for the physician. They were impressed and said they would sign a contract.

Instead of resting, Ruby asked more questions and tapped the answers into her computer.

"Who else should you communicate this program with?" (You want to involve as many others in the corporation as possible, right down to the administrative assistants and billing specialists).

"Would you like me to make this sales presentation to your staff? How about to any satellite offices?"

"Where shall we ship? And when?"

"Any special deadlines coming up that need to be met?"

"Now for the training sessions. When shall we start training you and your people? If we come to you it will cost about the same as if you come to us. Oh, why wait until next winter? We could do it next month and conduct our training sessions at the Lodge at North Star at Lake Tahoe?

"By the way. The price includes refreshers for new staff every quarter."

By the time the doctors walked away they were thoroughly involved in their new purchase, excited about its prospects, and making plans around it.

Think of the sound of a thud if they had been sold and the sales rep had simply moved on to make another sale. Imagine a big trout left flopping and helpless on the bank.

Axiom Thirty: Play with Patience and Caution

Fish on! Some hooked fish will sulk and wait, requiring much coaxing. Some run away hard, pulling backing from the reel with a singing fury. All trout resist in some way. Brake the trout's run with caution. Keep your rod tip high.

> *There's a period about six months after you get the new business that the honeymoon ends. You can count on it like clockwork. Be aware of it and plan for it.*
> —The late H. Devereaux Jennings, marketing manager
> Waterville Valley ski area

A Sale Never Ends

Any relationship is going to have some touch-and-go periods, especially during the beginning when you are trying to fit your service or product with a new customer.

It's like knowing how to play a trout. Too much tension and you'll snap the line. Know when to take up slack and when to let them run.

We are talking personalities and relationships, here. Chances are pretty good the person you sold the product to is not the one you will be dealing with in the after-sale.

For instances, after Ruby Custer sold the laser surgical equipment to the California eye surgeons, she had to work out billing procedures and mesh costs of the device and its support units into the standard billing fees of the surgical practice.

In this aspect Ruby dealt with a woman she called "Nurse Ratchet." This was an older woman, an office manager upon whom the doctors in the practice counted-on to coordinate the vital aspect of keeping them profitable.

Before she ever met Nurse Ratchet Ruby said to me, "She will be a challenge. This is a woman who has not been involved in process of purchasing the device. Its installation and use will create more work for her. She will have a learning curve to figure out how to operate it. She may have to train others. She will have to deal with new kinds of billing procedures and patient explanations. She may fear change."

Ruby's predictions proved correct. On their first meeting she sensed the office manager's resistance. Nurse Ratchet wanted to postpone the start-up, saying she didn't have time to become acquainted with the product. She said her staff was very busy. She said that the doctors didn't understand how overloaded they were.

Ruby sympathized. She had counted on this.

"Yes, I talked to your doctors about how difficult this might be for you. Start-ups are always a challenge. They assured me you were great at your job so I knew you'd be up to it. What I would like you to do is help me plan the training sessions at Lake Tahoe. They've agreed to give the staff a four day-weekend to take part. We'll hold morning training sessions. Afternoons you'll be own your own to enjoy Lake Tahoe and the casinos. Are you going to bring your husband?"

Ruby spent the next two weeks making frequent calls to the doctors and staff, always with something important to ask or with some news updating the sale. Even after the delivery of the product she took Nurse Ratchet to lunch regularly. She sent small gifts to the rest of the staff. The docs got gift certificates for fly fishing with a guide on the Walker River near Bridgeport. Ruby often called asking how things were going, were they satisfied with her product?

She maintained a presence after the sale and does to this day. It assures that she will get feedback on her product's use which she can use in future sales, and it assures that her customers are happy. Nurse Ratchet became Ruby's "friend inside." The practice has continued to be a re-purchaser of Ruby's products for several years now.

Be patient. Change can be difficult to embrace and some will run screaming from it. Others will bow graciously to its inevitability. As when playing a fish, Ruby was patient and cautious while coaxing Nurse Ratchet to accept a new product.

Axiom Thirty One: Bring Them Gently to the Net

The trout comes at last to hand, weary of its struggles, convinced of your powerful argument. Savor it, but celebrate the landing modestly, for you may loose him yet.

*Talk about those subjects you have had long in your mind,
and listen to what others say about subjects you have studied but recently.
Knowledge and timber shouldn't be much used till they are seasoned.*
—Oliver Wendell Holmes, *The Autocrat of the Breakfast Table*

Money Will Be Contentious

If there is a post-sale struggle with your new customer, it will likely be over money. The misunderstandings over dollars are like the last minute sounding of a trout, propelled by a final burst of energy in its attempt to shake the hook.

Once I had secured as a client the Flint Savings and Loan Company which had run a lengthy ad campaign seeking customers to open savings accounts.

We had agreed on the commissions to be paid, we had agreed on the budget of the campaign, the media we would use and the markets we would target. We signed a contract and I went to work.

I presented our first bill, which included a lot of money for production of television spots. It included the cost of writing the commercial, the director, camera man, sound man, props, studio, editing and so on.

"This isn't mine," said Mr. Flint, the owner, a sarcastic, gray-haired man with more than 35 years in the business. "It's yours."

"No. It's for your company's television spots," I explained, mystified.

"No way. That's a cost you pay out of your commissions."

Now we had to return to our contract. My recollection was that he was paying all production costs, traditional (but not universal) in most advertising and marketing agency contracts.

I was correct. The contract clearly stated the client would pay for production of all materials for placement on television or in other media.

"That's not what I did with my last agency," he growled. His face was turning the color of a brook trout's belly. "You want my business, you do business my way."

Do I hold him to the contract and alienate him as a client? Surely that would end the relationship. It might even result in litigation.

Instead I took him to lunch and tried for a compromise. I showed him exactly what our profit was in the production of the spots, and agreed to give him the spots at our cost. I also suggested we extend the use of these television commercials for a longer period of time, so that their one-time costs could be amortized over a longer period.

This was all it took. We kept the account for many years. He could have broken the line and dived away, but the sale stayed in the net.

Axiom Thirty Two: Practice Candor

Wet your hands. Keep your grip gentle but firm.

> *Being honest doesn't mean causing pain.*
> —Mr. Joseph Faye Hanson, my fourth grade school teacher

Care and Handling of a Tough Customer

Sometimes a trout is hard to take off the hook. He will thrash and beat against things and may hurt himself in the process. You must be firm but gentle.

And so it is with your customer when she begins demanding the extras in service and product that eat up time and money.

Early in my career I worked for a great sales account manager, Douglas Willey. He told me, "There is some dung you don't have to eat."

What he meant was that having good boundaries is important to your success in sales. It meant being unafraid to say no when the client is pushing for too much. But his use of the word "dung," rather than a more robust Anglo-Saxon noun implied a tact that I've tried to carry with me.

I had been working with Michael Whiting, a manufacturer of window casements and something of a bully when it came to extracting all the juice from those who worked for him. He was a pretty good customer, but now he was demanding more time than could possibly be justified, considering the budget we had been given to work with.

Now Whitely wanted me to man his booth at a trade convention in Denver, and he asked me to do this at no charge, as an unspoken demand for his doing business with us. I felt demeaned by this, as it was not in my job description for this client. I thought about it for a day, and then went to Michael Whitely.

"Mike, we need to make money on your business or the wheels fall off our little contract. I'll be glad to go to Denver if you'll pay me my regular hourly fee."

Whitely was the kind of businessman that always pushed for just a little extra from his vendors. I knew he wasn't going to pay me my hourly fee for this. He could get a temp for a lot less. And he did.

There was no need to be confrontational. A simple, good natured statement of facts prevented causing any pain to him or to me.

You do not have to people-please to stay in the sales business. Just remember that everyone needs to make a profit and that diplomacy is better than a tight grip on your ego and your wallet.

Axiom Thirty Three: Never Eat Your Customer

Trout are too valuable to eat. Care for them, love them, help them, and they may be caught again and again another day.

You can get anyone to buy a product once;
it's the repurchase rate that's important.
—Anonymous, business meeting at Procter and Gamble Group of Companies.

You can shear a sheep over and over again, but you can only skin him once.
--Joseph McCune Ure, Connor Sport Court International

Good Profits, Little-By-Slowly

Your best customer is the customer you already have. Like a released trout, he can be caught over-and-over again.

It can cost 10 times more to get a new customer than to keep an existing one. Not only that, many of my customers have become good friends and I want to keep them as friends.

If you make a fair profit in your transactions you can continue to make those transactions into the foreseeable future.   If you gouge your client for big returns, he will go away and will not return.

Deal with your customer as you do with a trout and they will return to your net another day.

Last But Not Least: Always Provide a Service

Always view your work in sales as a service to others. Does your fishing provide a service to trout? Yes, you are helping a trout learn to avoid a rough cast or a poor fly. He becomes more wary. The trout in your river become more genetically robust as selectivity takes place. This creates a greater challenge for fishermen. He makes you into a better fisher.

It is the fly fishing experience, not the weight in our creel, by which we measure our pleasure.

>If fishing is a religion, fly fishing is high church.
>—Tom Brokaw

Amen.

www.ingramcontent.com/pod-product-compliance
Lightning Source LLC
Chambersburg PA
CBHW081846170526
45167CB00007B/2915